naked thoughts

Poetry by

quandra

© 2003 by quandra. All rights reserved.

No part of this book may be reproduced,
stored in a retrieval system, or transmitted by any
means, electronic, mechanical, photocopying,
recording, or otherwise, without written permission
from the author.

ISBN: 1-4107-7332-9 (e-book)
ISBN: 1-4107-7331-0 (Paperback)

This book is printed on acid free paper.

1stBooks - rev. 07/10/03

statement of faith

I worship the one true God who co-exists eternally as Father, Son, and Holy Spirit (Matt. 28:19)

I proclaim Christ's deity and His lordship over all (John 1:1,14; Phil. 2:5-11)

I believe in the divine inspiration and final authority of God's Word (2 Tim. 3:16,17)

I am an evangelical Christian that believes in salvation by grace alone through faith alone in Christ alone (Acts 4:12; Eph. 2:8)

I am a Spirit-filled Christian who relies on the Holy Spirit to make me effective in ministry and witness for Christ (Acts 1:8; Eph. 5:18)

I am a Spirit-led Christian who welcomes the orderly exercise of all spiritual gifts which exalt Christ and edify the church (1 Cor. 14:26; 1 Pe. 4:10)

I yield to the Holy Spirit as He works in me to cultivate godliness and disciplined living (Gal. 5:22-23; 2 Cor. 7:1)

table of contents

introduction vii
dedication. ix
poetry disclaimer xi
warm springs boulevard 1
blessed body bought by blood 3
just believe 5
welcome to the service 8
do it, get it 11
the way we do 14
holiest thing in hell 16
it's time to rally 18
preeeach 21
living epistle 25
love is 28
are you ready? or just willing? 31
christmas story 33
lovelocks 36
men's day (at new hope church of God in Christ) ..37
friends like you 39
for you 40
friendship 43
rough side of the mountain 45
so small 46
independence 47
church dress sequence but no sense 49
angry man 52
saved? from what? 54

v

two fools	56
forgiveness	58
love letter	61
careful	64
my lover	67
a baby	69
virtue won't hurt you	71
unGodly matrimony	74
single lady	77
my times are in God's hands	80
quandra's affirmation against grasshopper mentality	82
imperfect but on purpose	85
the good shepherd	88
Holy Ghost	90
fully persuaded	92
to the defeated	94
so thirsty	97
still waters	99
ain't no harm	100
come home	102
memphis anointing	103
testify	106
what is joy?	108
pick me up	109
then	113
contact author	115
what I've learned	116
about the author	117

introduction

why did i write a book of poetry? well, the answer lies in a search i started about 3 years ago. before ever writing a poem of my own, i searched for poetry with which i could identify. i was searching for edgy, Christ-centered poetry. i could find edgy poetry. i could find Christ-centered poetry. but, i wanted to find one poet that conceived the two into a unique style of writing that candidly depicted the dynamics of the Christian life. i have yet to find a published poet who has achieved that unique conception. therefore, my search continues.

there are, however, four poets that have impressed me deeply: tupac shakur, tonye joiner, maya angelou, and blare from los angeles. tupac, in his collection of poems entitled <u>the rose that grew from concrete</u>, exhibits a beautiful spirit of emotion and honesty. tupac's poetry is the simplest, most heart-warming poetry i have ever read. tonye joiner, the author of <u>my people, my poetry</u>, is the first poet i ever saw who did more than recite her poetry: she performs it. maya angelou, with her beautifully powerful voice, displays more rhythm and song in her poetry than any poet i know. finally, blare from los angeles, has a pure heart. i met blare at an open mic poetry event at west angeles church of God in Christ. i love her very conscious rhymes that admonish and encourage. she is a great thinking poet. these four individuals represent the small group of poets who have influenced my perception and understanding of poetry. their work inspires me to write my own.

    what is poetry? in my opinion, poetry is a collection of naked thoughts. there are many types of writers: journalists, essayists, and novelists just to name a few. non-poet writers clothe their writing with sophisticated format and accessorize their writing with punctuation, cohesive themes, grammar, and plots. they dress their writing beautifully. but, poetry writing allows me to be completely free from such formalities. i can abandon punctuation, grammar, cohesive themes, and plots. my thoughts can roam naked from page to page exposed for the purpose of showing my kindred spirits they are not so strange for thinking what they think or feeling what they feel.

this book is dedicated to and inspired by the long list of folk who challenge my Christian love and put me in a place where God can further purify my surrendered heart.
thank you.

x

poetry disclaimer

my poetry is not a book of theology and beliefs but feelings and thoughts at random points in my life. my poetry reflects what i feel but does not always reflect what i believe.

sometimes, my emotions betray my intellect depending on how reality affects me. i am a Christian but this is not "gospel" poetry. This is just quandra's poetry.

And the God of all grace, who called you to his eternal glory in Christ, after you have suffered a little while, will himself restore you and make you strong, firm and steadfast.
1 Peter 5:10

naked thoughts

warm springs boulevard

on sunday
if you had been looking for me
i was at 9248 E. 14th street
among God's folk
blessed with new hope
but then God moved me to a different oasis
of fruitful service and new faces

God gave me warm springs
to comfort and nourish me
here in this south bay community
and God has revealed to me that on this side of
eternity
healthy doesn't mean perfection
but rather a recognition
of our lack of perfection
along this sojourn to spiritual maturity
God gave me warms springs to comfort and nourish
me
i haven't lost hope in that new hope
i just need to take heed to
the Spirit's leading me
to these warm springs folk
in this new oasis filled with new faces

i know finding a spiritual family is so hard
that's why i'm so glad God led me to warm springs
boulevard

quandra

The body is a unit, though it is made up of many parts; and though all its parts are many, they form one body. So it is with Christ. ...Now you are the body of Christ, and each one of you is a part of it.
I Corinthians 12:12,27

naked thoughts

blessed body bought by blood

prophets preachers prayerful people

singing, slaying, saving, seeking

together take time to testify

every effort edifies

quandra

We live by faith, not by sight.
II Corinthians 5:7

just believe

if God is omnibenevolent, why do bad things happen and good people get the boot
if God is omnipresent, why couldn't he stop eve before she ate the fruit
if God is omniscient, why did he even create the tree with the forbidden fruit

because of all these questions, your faith is mute

why

why

why

now, God has a few questions for you

how many stars have you hung in sky?

how many heavens have you stretched out light-years wide?

how many worlds have you formed and held in the palm of your hand

quandra

now don't lie

none

none

none

let God be God
we cannot understand it all
i will offer this relief
let God be God and
you just believe

naked thoughts

So, because you are lukewarm— neither hot nor cold— I am about to spit you out of my mouth.
Revelation 3:16

quandra

welcome to the service

cold church
misplaced amens
funeral fans
folk looking' funny
when it's time to give that money
ain't in the Spirit
Wasn't even near it
cold church

lukewarm church
no prayer, no fasting
are you saved?
calm down
just asking
salvation is more than ceremony
why are your services oh-so boring
so let me suggest you hurry up and shout
unto God with a voice of triumph
Before God gets angry and spits you out

hot church
can you feel the fire
come to take us higher
thank God for this oil
fell on good soil
did you see that dove
sent through grace by love

naked thoughts

to cultivate this place
plant some mustard seed faith
hot church

quandra

Jesus looked at them and said, "With man this is impossible, but with God all things are possible."
Matthew 19:26

naked thoughts

do it, get it

do it, get it
you can
do it, do it
get it, get it

if you want to go to college
go
whether it's harvard or the local community college
do it, get it
ain't much to it but to
do it, do it
get it, get it

if you want a new car
buy it
whether it's a lexus or a ford
do it, get it
ain't much to it but to
do it, do it
get it, get it

if you want that promotion
earn it
whether you have a degree or a ged
do it, get it
ain't much to it but to
do it, do it
get it, get it

quandra

i pray as if it all depends on God
knowing He has already walked out my path
long before i even asked
for the provisions that line up with his visions
but then i work like it all depends on me
knowing bread from heaven won't just fall into my hand
i need to push and press to make it to my promised land
knowing God's grace will sustain me for the distance

so i can do it
i can get it
knowing ain't much to it but to
do it, do it
get it, get it

naked thoughts

A cheerful heart is good medicine, but a crushed
spirit dries up the bones.
Proverbs 17:22

quandra

the way we do

i was shocked and amazed
when that crazed psychotic wildebeest
threatened to spit on me
at that convention service over the summer
and then told me to comb my hair
looking like something from a wild lair
we found humor in that episode with that particular
fool
but don't look so confused
this is just the way we do

i almost bust a gut
laughing at that nut
who threatened to cut
me simply 'cause i said she looked a little dirty
surprisingly, we laughed at that too
but don't look so confused
'cause this is just the way we do

and the saga continues
different venues
episode after episode
of one long hilarious joke
but don't look so confused
you know this is just
the way we do
dedicated to jeremy and montree

naked thoughts

> No, a man is a Jew if he is one inwardly; and circumcision is circumcision of the heart, by the Spirit, not by the written code. Such a man's praise is not from men, but from God.
> Romans 2:29

quandra

holiest thing in hell

my lips slightly moistened with clear gloss, but of course no lipstick

that would be sinful

My skirt flowed straight down to my ankles, but of course no split

that would be sinful

my lobes, wrists, and neck were bare, but of course no jewelry

that would be sinful

but when the last trumpet sounded, my countenance fell

my heart was uncircumcised

i was the holiest thing in hell

naked thoughts

My prayer is not for them alone. I pray for those who will believe in me through their message, that all of them may be one
John 17:20-21b

quandra

it's time to rally

babylon is rising
and jerusalem does not yet have that peace plan
so it's no time for compromising
'cause we can't drive to heaven in the church-
sponsored van
i say it's time to rally

some get so heady
and stumble over such petty
foolish things

like
sister what-not spoke like she didn't even want to
greet me
and she never says amen when i preach
and look now she's sitting in my assigned seat
we must focus on more important things

our lives are only vapors rising to eternity
and all that i do on this earth affects my heavenly
standing
so if you asked me
i say it's time to rally

naked thoughts

no one in church should have to praise alone
carried off to some praise room
so their praise won't disturb you
if praise to God disturbs you
perhaps you should stay home
no one in church should have to praise God alone

rally for that greater common cause
orphans
widows
missions
witnessing
God's commissions
to save the world

remember God said
the first shall be last
and the last shall be first
so let's get over our titles
and prestigious positions
let's rally
let's rally
let's rally
to fulfill God's commissions

quandra

Therefore once more I will astound these people with
wonder upon wonder; the wisdom of the wise will
perish, the intelligence of the intelligent will vanish.
Isaiah 29:14

preeeach

sorry
i'm not a
take it to the bridge
hit a refrain
adlib and change keys
kind of speaker

i'm just a content-based
gospel in your face
edify my people
kind of speaker

but hey kudos to the preachers and teachers
who can entertain with a dance, stomp, and twirl
hold their ear while steadying the mic
amidst key changes
all while recalling the story of daniel in the lion's den
creatively relating it to modern-day sin
kudos
if that's how your anointing flows

but i'm just not a
take it to the bridge
hit a refrain
adlib and change keys
kind of speaker

quandra

i'm just a content-based
gospel in your face
edify my people
kind of speaker

i love it when the congregation gets really quiet
'cause them i'm assured
you've heard every God-given word
it doesn't hurt my feelings when you don't say
amen or stand
it's not my intent to gain a fan
i'm just trying to edify that man
woman
girl
and Boy
i just want to know
do you have the Holy Ghost
the power you need to say no
i just want to help you grow
in the Word

that's how we edify and build each other's faith
daily i face two enemies attacking me
satan's temptations
and the lust of my own flesh
i confess
i need a gospel-word to get out of this mess

naked thoughts

so i'm just not a
take it to the bridge
hit a refrain
adlib and change keys
kind of speaker

i'm a content-based
gospel in your face
edify my people
kind of speaker

quandra

We are therefore Christ's ambassadors, as though
God were making his appeal through us. We implore
you on Christ's behalf: Be reconciled to God
II Corinthians 5:20

living epistle

people are watching us
so let's be that 67th book of the bible
'cause they're holding us liable
for the credibility of christianity

there are certain obvious no-no's
we should avoid
when professing Christ to be our Lord

right around the time you start preaching
you should not be caught drinking yourself drunk
with a little hennessy in your coke
you can't free me from the yoke
on which you yourself choke

if you're an evangelist teacher commissioned to save the lost
you might want to abstain from
gossipping at work with your boss
try to minimize the souls you bludgeon with your untamed tongue
while on your mission to bring souls into God's kingdom

quandra

if you're an unmarried teen singing in the choir
you might want to avoid have tyronne's lust child
your friends at school won't hear your testimony
if from what they see they think your professed
salvation is nothing more than phoney

folk are eager to use our hypocrisy
as their excuse for apostasy
they're watching us
to see if we're true forms of godliness or just winds of
doctrine
meant only to manipulate women and men
out of their money to fund the devilment of clergy
men

so while it is true we are not perfect yet
there are vices in this life
from which we should abstain
so folk don't blaspheme the name
of our Lord Jesus Christ

naked thoughts

By this all men will know that you are my disciples,
if you love one another.
John 13:35

quandra

love is

without shame
i confess i am a christian
so i understand i am to love all men and all women

but frankly speaking
there are folk who lack maturity and intellect so
greatly
it's scary
and i just do not enjoy their company
which makes me wonder what love is
before i can commit to show this
i must have a concept of what love is

if there are those whose company i simply do not
enjoy
then love must be more than
mushy sentiment
or the act of being affectionate
so perhaps love is some sentiment plus trust

but frankly speaking
there are folk so triflin' and sneaky
trust is the very last sentiment flowing from me
to them
is this a sin?

naked thoughts

so perhaps love is more than trust
more than sentiment
perhaps love is compassion
to be at one in suffering with another
no matter their color
everyone is my sister and brother
because we share the same father

yes, i can handle this with the help of God's Spirit
i can love all men and all women
knowing love is more than sentiment
more than feelings
'cause sometimes your aura is so offensive
my feelings would and could
cause me to treat you contrary to how i know should
but love is a decision
to be concerned for you
a decision
to be a partner in suffering with you
a decision
to be an intercessor in prayer for you
yes, i can handle this
i can commit to show this
what
love is

quandra

For you know very well that the day of the Lord will
come like a thief in the night.
1 Thessalonians 5:2

naked thoughts

are you ready? or just willing?

if God cracked the sky right now
and Christ rode down upon a cloud
would you be ready for judgment
somewhere out for lunch
with your gossiping buddy
getting the latest dirt
thinking it won't hurt
'cause you'll be in church
on Sunday,
so every other day is your day
because you can always repent on sunday
but let me ask if i may
what if Christ returns on saturday

quandra

Father, if you are willing, take this cup from me; yet
not my will, but yours be done.
Luke 22:42

naked thoughts

christmas story

although it isn't cute and maybe even gory
this is the real christmas story
no stockings
no bells
no santa
no elves

Jesus was born
born to die
so you and i
could have life and that more abundantly

the anointed son of God
He was to be our savior
make us spotless
give us divine favor

they lifted Him up
so He could draw all men
nailed to a tree
bearing all our sin
beaten with many lashes
so i needn't pray in sackcloth and ashes

quandra

He was
spit on
stoned
lied on
and de-throned

but
then the veil was rent
that's why He was sent
not only born to die
but born to reconcile

although it isn't cute and maybe even gory
this is the real christmas story

naked thoughts

During the entire period of his vow of separation no razor may be used on his head. He must be holy until the period of his separation to the Lord is over; he must let the hair of his head grow long.
Numbers 6:5

quandra

lovelocks

i call mine lovelocks no dreadlocks
for they're not dreadful but are a head full
of dedication
while in consecration

holy and set aside
to God i will draw nigh
a symbol of vanities forsaken
you need not agree with the path i have taken

i won't talk about your weaves and perms
won't preach about how they demean and burn
i've accepted what i've discerned
we'll each be what we have learned

men's day (at new hope church of God in Christ)

it's men's day
that glorious day when we gather to appreciate
these brothas who share our pigment
but are not in prison
i know sistas and brothas who think every black church
is crooked and shady
but this is men's day
when we gather to appreciate these black men
who are not entangled with sin

it's men's day
a time to appreciate
elder byrd slapping the bass
deacon bates with the offering plates
pastor starks singing his guitars
james kevin beating the drums
elder chavis streaming down that aisle
with his 4 black men sons, that makes me smile
and you can tell andre's little girls
mean more to him than this whole wide world

it's men day
so let's be careful to appreciate
these brothas
despite their being late
to the service today

quandra

some ladies might feel our black man's image lacks
credibility, stability, and or anything Godly
but if you ask me
I say here at new hope
these brothas are reviving new hope for all black men
cause this men's day
is a time to appreciate
some beautiful black men who are not entangled
with sin
these brothas who share our pigment
i just want to say
thank you
for this
men's day

naked thoughts

friends like you

i have no need for
enemies
because you're faithful
to betray me
distrust me
mistreat me
misunderstand me
tease and leave me
then lie and say
you
love me
need me
intend the best for me
and never meant to hurt me
with friends like you
i have no need for
enemies

quandra

for you

can you feel me
do you really hear me
i wonder if you feel this
do you really hear this

it's amazing that i
surrounded by
people can still
feel
lonely
not alone
but lonely
'cause no one really feels me
or listens well enough to hear me

sometimes i wonder what
i want from you
then i think maybe
it's not fair
maybe i want too much
maybe i don't give enough

i want someone who will
trust me
forgive me
talk with me
listen to me
be affectionate

naked thoughts

but maybe this isn't fair
maybe i want too much
perhaps i don't give enough

so i alone must
feel myself
understand myself
encourage myself
and never expect your help

sometimes i get tired of being
the only one keeping me company
but if i don't love me
who will
if i don't feel me
who will
if i don't encourage me
will you

i'm thinking no
'cause up until now
you haven't let it show
it being love
and words are not enough
show me
so i don't feel so lonely

can you feel me
do you really hear me
i wonder if you feel this
if you even really hear this

quandra

If an enemy were insulting me, I could endure it; if a foe were raising himself against me, I could hide from him. But it is you, a man like myself, my companion, my close friend, with whom I once enjoyed sweet fellowship as we walked with the throng at the house of God.
Psalms 55:12-14

friendship

what had been my greatest blessing
became my hardest lesson
what had been my sweetest pleasure and joy
became a sinister plot and ploy
against me
to hurt me
and to think, i thought you loved me
you weren't full of love but envy
and grew resentful when you realized you couldn't
be me like me
my safe haven egypt became my personal plantation
you had me making recantations
for every promise made in hasty infatuation
my laughter and hopes for happily ever after
are no more
and that was a heavy cross i bore
i'm speaking only of friendship
how you can become so enamored with someone
you've just met
and not really even know them yet
so infatuated with this new friend
left confused and hurt when it comes to an end
and just when i think it's all an unfair plan against
me
God gives me another friend
and another
and another
all the same pleasures and pains again

quandra

> Why are you downcast, O my soul? Why so disturbed within me? Put your hope in God, for I will yet praise him, my Savior and my God.
> Psalm 43:5

rough side of the mountain

my sadness
because of this madness
always leads me to repentance
'cause i just can't make sense
of why things fall apart
though i struggle with all my heart
to put God first
he allows life to hurt
i hit my knees
about to make pleas
not really knowing what to say
just wishing there were an easier way

quandra

so small

how does it feel to be so small
to find a reason to be offended
in any and all situations
in a constant state of agitation

are you even aware of your own faults
are you aware that you posses every negative
quality you put on them and me
do you annoy yourself as much as you
annoy everybody else

late at night, right before you drift into sleep
that time of the night when we all ponder
most sincerely
what do you really think
of yourself
and how you relate to everybody else

how does it feel

to be

so small

independence

if you're living in your mother's house
and eating your mother's food
you don't really have the right
to complain about your mother's rules

independence is expensive 'cause bills never cease to come
but at least then you have your own freedom

if you don't like your mother's house
and you're tired of your mother's food
tired of your mother's rules

finish school

move out

make your living

independence is earned not given

quandra

You, then, who teach others, do you not teach
yourself?
Romans 2:21a

naked thoughts

church dress sequence but no sense

i'm so tired of no-knowledge-having church folk
who could not quote
a verse to save their life
telling me what's wrong and right
coming to church with all that goofy sequence and
that big study bible that they haven't read in
months despite their leadership role at church
trying to tell me,
"darling, do you think the Lord would be pleased
with those
painted toe nails
those blue jeans
that lipstick
or that jazz music you like to play"

all i ever want to say is
"church folk, do you think the Lord is
pleased with
your lustful thoughts and desires
your single pursuit of your own happiness
your faithful reading of your horoscope
your fits of rage when setting other folk straight
your envy and jealously
manifest in your constant critiquing of me"

quandra

"so, despite the fruit of the Spirit deeply rooted and
maturing in me
and the fruit of the flesh freely festering in you
the trivialities of
nail polish
music
jeans
and lipstick
top your ridiculous list
of important issues?"

naked thoughts

Do not make friends with a hot-tempered man, do not associate with one easily angered, or you may learn his ways and get yourself ensnared.
Proverbs 22:24-25

quandra

angry man

yes, we all know it's not your fault
nothing is your fault
you just got caught
in between bad timing and other people's problems
right
but, of course, nothing is ever your fault

you can't get decent work
'cause your ancestors were enslaved only 400 years
ago
so everyone should understand and know
why that glass ceiling is just too low
for you to go
beyond bagging items at the local grocery store

you can't love your wife the way she deserves
because of your daddy's and his daddy's hurts
that were imposed on you way back when you were
in pre-school
so everyone should understand and know
that you can't show any love and affection without a
verbal or physical blow to your wife's jaw leaving
just a few teeth loose

but, of course, none of this is your fault
you just got caught
in between bad timing and other people's problems
right

naked thoughts

Do not let your mouth lead you into sin. And do not protest to the temple messenger, "My vow was a mistake." Why should God be angry at what you say and destroy the work of your hands?
Ecclesiastes 5:6

quandra

saved? from what?

you say you're saved
and Jesus is your savior
but what changes have you made
did he change your heart
but not your behavior

explain to me
how you can be
saved from sin
while you're yet in
that same predicament
when God says you must repent
still lying
still smoking
still clubbing
still sexing
still gambling
still scheming
still trying to live saved
without actually
living holy

but faith without works is dead
find a healthy church
where you can be fed
one that's led
by God's Spirit
Lord, let all who have an ear to hear
hear it

naked thoughts

For it is God's will that by doing good you should silence the ignorant talk of foolish men.
1 Peter 2:15

quandra

two fools

no matter who i complain to
or how i pray
no matter how i change to suit you
or what i carefully choose to say
you two
will be
the same two
fools
doing what you do best
yes, being pests

annoying
aggravating
irritating
and always instigating

two high priests of your own
pretentious citadels
but now
it doesn't phase me anymore
'cause i know no matter what i do
you two
will be
the same two
fools

naked thoughts

When a man's ways are pleasing to the Lord, he
makes even his enemies live at peace with him.
Proverbs 16:7

quandra

forgiveness

my bitterness towards you
became a discomfort in my own

spirit
       soul
              and body

your offense towards me is just a memory
a trite, trivial tendency
but i could not have peace
with the memory replaying within me

and i need a way to get it out
70 times 7 times i am to forgive
let by-gones be by-gones, live and let live
i am to find it in my heart to grant you a pardon
so my jargon can become sincere concern and love
for you
but what exactly do i do
to rid myself of this bitterness towards you

so i know i need to forgive you
not out of obligation or self-imposed condemnation
but i know i need to forgive you
and the Spirit of the Lord has told me exactly what
to do

naked thoughts

while i can acknowledge that i've been hurt
i need to remove the memory
of your offense towards me
by pulling down that stronghold
of that thing that holds me strong

i will extend my hand towards you
not for relationship
not for any deep fellowship
but to do all that i can just to bless you
expecting no reciprocation or acceptance
for my repentance
towards you
for i can see
that forgiveness is a one-way street

praying that God anoint me with the strength,
power, and love
to rise above
the memory of your offense towards me

quandra

Daughters of Jerusalem, I charge you by the gazelles
and by the does of the field: Do not arouse or awaken
love until it so desires.
Song of Songs 2:7

naked thoughts

love letter

i want someone to write a love letter to
could it be you
were you sent to me
to be my lion and i your lioness
i want someone to write a love letter to
could it be you

you definitely have the look
i love men with
hot chocolate skin
wide shoulders, large hands, full lips
with that confidence that says they love
the skin they're in

you definitely have the style
preppy intellectual
with those polo shirts and khakis
cool-rimmed spectacles
with that little leather case for your keys

you definitely have the mind
a literate thinker
a brother unafraid
to defend his position against a lady with an
opinion

quandra

    but do you have my Savior
    faith in God through
    the Lord Jesus Christ
    by God's Holy Spirit

    well, then
    my search continues
    i want someone to write a love letter to
    i thought it could be you
    i thought you might have been sent to me
    to be my lion and i your lioness
    but we don't agree
    spiritually
    so you could not have been sent for me

naked thoughts

Flee the evil desires of youth, and pursue righteousness, faith, love and peace, along with those who call on the Lord out of a pure heart.
II Timothy 2:22

quandra

careful

there's this guy chris at work
he's so cute
it's difficult not to flirt
i imagined in my mind's eye
what a date with him would be like

he's not saved but he's so nice
his lack of salvation won't really matter
right?
a date is just a date
right?

we could go out for a movie
then dinner
then he'd take me home
i'd invite him in
with no intent to sin
though
he'd just come in
for some hot chocolate and whipped cream
while we innocently stare at the tv screen
really enjoying each other's company
innocently

then he'll set down his cup of hot chocolate
look at me
with sinful intent in his eyes

naked thoughts

and start spewing those familiar lies
like
girl you are so fine
i think you and i
could have something special
just trust me
i'm for real shorty

then that sharp taste of fear will be in my mouth
'cause i'll realize
i'm about 20 miles south
from the center of God's will
2 kisses and 1 caress
from allowing my flesh
to fornicate
so perhaps
a date is not just a date

because one date
can turn a virgin
into an expecting mother
a young brother
into an inadequate father
placing ourselves in the face of unnecessary temptations
for the sake of fleeting, unsatisfying infatuations

in my effort to avoid satan's lake
for my soul's sake
i will always remember
a date is not just a date

quandra

Yet, I hold this against you: You have forsaken your
first love.
Revelation 2:4

naked thoughts

my lover

i'm a single young lady
i live alone
no boyfriends phone
i'm just a single young lady
but i do have a lover
who loves deeper than those under the cover

my lover raises the sun to brighten my day
breathes life into my senses so i can be on my way
gives me power
so i can tower above satan's temptations
like fornication
masturbation
contemplations of the black islamic nation
and every other -ation
some saints avoid in conversation

i'm a single young lady
i live alone
no boyfriends phone
i'm just a single young lady
but i do have a lover
who loves deeper than those under the cover

my lover didn't put on a tux and take me to the prom
He put on mortal flesh and reconciled me back to
God

quandra

my lover doesn't walk me to my door and lay a kiss
on my lips
while fondling my hips
no He put a sanctified stride in my sanctified legs
to help keep me chaste
and anointed me with a holy fragrance that has
dog repellent in it
so brothas never step to me with lines like
can I hit it

yeah, i'm just a single young lady
i live alone
no boyfriends phone
i'm just a single young lady
but i do have a lover
and he loves me so much deeper than those under the
cover

a baby

the beauty of child birth amazes me
i can't wait to be
a door of life for one of God's chosen
to walk from conception inside God's mind
through me
into time
for me to steward
until eternity
the whole process sounds beautifully divine

i don't mean to romanticize or trivialize
how you ladies agonize at delivery time
but you have to admit
the glory outweighs the pain
which would explain
why women suffer the labor
and then
get pregnant again
again
and again

quandra

Because I love your commands more than gold, more
than pure gold, and because I consider all your
precepts right, I hate every wrong path.
Psalms 119:127-128

naked thoughts

virtue won't hurt you

some girls view virtue as a stigma to avoid
gotta be cool while chasing that bad boy
they want to be experience
cannot see the danger in this

never held hands
never been kissed
never been held
never had sex
can't you see you're blessed

some girls see virtue as a stigma to avoid
dropping mama's advice while chasing that bad boy
got spring fever
no clue he's gonna leave her

just remember in december
when alone with your new baby
just maybe
you were only soil
that he meant to spoil
dropping his wild seeds
by making you weak in your knees

when you give him what he wants…only known him for two months
he doesn't want you anymore

quandra

heard him calling you a whore
remember before december
those girls who drop their virtue and just a fall into
bed
are never the ones those bad boys wed

naked thoughts

Do not be yoked together with unbelievers. For what do righteousness and wickedness have in common? Or what fellowship can light have with darkness?
II Corinthians 6:14

quandra

unGodly matrimony

satan does not try to woe me with a pitchfork, horns, a tight red suit
or any other myths
but he comes with good looks, charm, and a form of righteousness

but I must pray and watch
because unGodly matrimony is just a prelude to alimony
and sex with a sinner man is not a form of witnessing
i know satan will never leave me but then again he'll never love me

in the midst of my compromise
i tell myself such lies
as i am drawing him to Christ
i'm saving this brother's life

if this were true and pleasing to our Lord
that would make God my pimp
and me his holy whore

no

naked thoughts

God is my heavenly father
we are all to be his
chaste
virtuous
daughters

so i will pray and watch
because unGodly matrimony is just a prelude to
alimony
and sex with a sinner man is not a form of
witnessing
i know satan will never leave me but then again he'll
never love me

quandra

For I know the plans I have for you, declares the Lord, plans to prosper you and not to harm you, plans to give you hope and a future
Jeremiah 29:11

single lady

are you a single lady
struggling against your singlehood
thinking
"if only i could
be married
'cause i should
be a mommy
then i would
be happy"

instead
take your single life
and offer it to God as a sacrifice
all the extra time you have
all the extra money you have
all the extra love you have
offer it to God
through
volunteer work
church work
and career work
get your education
in this blessed time of consecration

live life to the absolute fullest
do all the things you love to do
be all the things you want to be

quandra

serve God in Christ to the fullest
meet eternity with no regrets

and even if we don't get husbands in this life
i'm assured that eternity will be worth the sacrifice

naked thoughts

There is a time for everything, and a season for every
activity under heaven
Ecclesiastes 3:1

quandra

my times are in God's hands

if i humble myself down
God will lift me up

if i stand at the back of the line
God will walk me to the front

i let God, in his sovereignty,
direct and guide me
because only he can see
all that i can and should be

naked thoughts

We saw the Nephilim there (the descendants of Anak come from the Nephilim). We seemed like grasshoppers in our own eyes, and we looked the same to them.
Numbers 13:33

quandra

quandra's affirmation against grasshopper mentality

i am not a grasshopper
i don't need to be anxious
i will eat the fruit
i've been grafted into that vine
my blessings are mine
and yours belong to you

secular women who justify their sin
despise and deride me
because at 23
i still possess my virginity
my lack of intimacy
with a man
is a testament of what i am
a princess
a lioness
more than just a form of godliness

i don't want to barely make it to heaven
still scraping leaven
from my teeth
given to me
by those who lead away silly women too heavy laden
with sin
to distinguish a wolf from one of God's men
i live with a sense of urgency

naked thoughts

excited about eternity
sanctified and holy
in my

spirit
       soul
              and body

i am not a grasshopper
i don't need to be anxious
i will eat the fruit
i've been grafted into that vine
my blessings are mine
and yours belong to you

quandra

Before I formed you in the womb I knew you, before you were born I set you apart; I appointed you as a prophet to the nations.
Jeremiah 1:5

naked thoughts

imperfect but on purpose

man credits chance and happenstance
for my existence
man says after the big bang and evolution
cells and molecules met accidentally
to form me
but I know my God made me purposefully
well aware I exist imperfectly, with faults of my own
aplenty
but I know God made me on purpose
man's theories contradict this
nevertheless, God made me on purpose

my face is not perfectly proportioned
my bank account is not blessed with fortune
my mind is not endowed with exceptional
intelligence
my body lacks hourglass measurements
nevertheless
God made me on purpose
yes, quandra t. mcgrue
stands before you
imperfect but purposefully made
Holy Ghost filled and saved
to fulfill God's ordained purpose for my life
by submitting to him through his Spirit by Christ

quandra

right now, what i really want to do
is to encourage you to never let low self-esteem make you blue
'cause you were made on purpose too

naked thoughts

I am the good shepherd. The good shepherd lays down his life for the sheep.
John 10:14

quandra

the good shepherd

everywhere i'm going
He's already been
opening doors before me
so i don't have to sin
removing obstacles that i never see
so i can walk in the Spirit consistently
because the good shepherd walks
before me

naked thoughts

But, the Counselor, the Holy Spirit, whom the Father will send in my name, will teach you all things and will remind you of everything I have said to you.
John 14:26

quandra

Holy Ghost

some wonder and wander
    what is the Holy Ghost

some question and ponder
    this is the part feared most

some reason while gawking
    what is the point of this tongue-talking?

but we're not drunk as you suppose
there's no wine hidden in our clothes

He is the third person of the Trinity, for me and you, sent to

        comfort
        guide
        search the deep things on our behalf
        intercede
        seal
        indwell
        so back to the question you asked

what is the Holy Ghost?

i think by now you might see

the question should not be what? but who?

the third person of the Trinity here for me and you

naked thoughts

Therefore, my dear friends, as you have always obeyed— not only in my presence, but now much more in my absence— continue to work out your salvation with fear and trembling, for it is God who works in you to will and to act according to his good purpose.
Philippians 2:12-13

quandra

fully persuaded

some days i get tired of
trying to convince myself that
suffering is a good thing
a necessary thing
that strengthens me
just tired and not on fire
i'm tired of dying all the day for Christ's sake
counted as a sheep
for the slaughter
satan pushes so hard
i'm running for the altar
then i realize this is one of satan's tricks
that killer, thief, and destroyer only wants me sin-sick

when i'm suffering i hate it
but i am fully and wholly persuaded
that nothing
no trials
no frustrations
no fiery darts
no evil imaginations
shall ever separate me
won't let satan take me
no never separate me
from the redeeming love of Christ

naked thoughts

Therefore, there is now no condemnation for those who are in Christ Jesus, because through Christ Jesus the law of the Spirit of life set me free from the law of sin and death.
Romans 8:1-2

quandra

to the defeated

in sackcloth and ashes
Lord
i'm embarrassed to even ask this

i've messed up again
familiar hang up
same tired sin

as i lay at your feet
contrite heart
broken spirit
one request, advocate, please hear it

restore my peace
revive and
forgive me
daily

but wait
let's not be defeated
not daily

if we read only Romans at 7
we'd think we could sin
and still get to heaven
but we must read the next chapter
if we want to make it at the rapture

naked thoughts

chapter 8 says to walk after the Spirit
not after the flesh
for it is the law of the Spirit that frees us from the
law of sin and death
the law of the Spirit
truth and purity
helping me to live holy
daily

quandra

Jesus answered, "Everyone who drinks this water will be thirsty again, but whoever drinks the water I give him will never thirst. Indeed, the water I give him will become in him a spring of water welling up to eternal life.
John 4:13-14

naked thoughts

so thirsty

like the samaritan woman
i went to the well of life
and met Christ
while seeking water to satisfy the
thirsting of my soul
and truly make me whole

this personal salvation
proven by archaeological
excavations and other such confirmations
is the living water
from Christ
welling up in me reaching to eternity
and thank God
'cause I was sooo thirsty

quandra

But God chose the foolish things of the world to shame the wise; God chose the weak things of the world to shame the strong. He chose the lowly things of this world and the despised things—and the things that are not—to nullify the things that are, so that no one may boast before him.
I Corinthians 1:27-29

still waters

mary
just a poor unknown peasant girl
but she birthed the savior of this world

jeremiah
just a humble child
but so full of God's word
his bones were on fire

moses
just a quiet boy who stuttered
he was scared
but he led God's children
and we all know how they fared

so don't discount the quiet, unknown, humble ones
those ones who seldom act or speak
are those used by God most powerfully
because God knows
still waters
run
so deep

quandra

ain't no harm

full of compromise
telling yourself lies
you let satan into your head
stayed too long
now your soul is dead
thought satan was your friend
but he just wants you full of sin

full of compromise
too late now though
i can already see the flies
swarming around your reprobate mind

ain't no harm
that's what you said
but look at you now
your soul is dead
feeling all alone
and full of dead man's bones

reprobate mind 'cause you didn't heed the signs
conscience is seared with the heat of satan's lies
now you're destined for the lake of fire
told yourself lies
full of compromise
too late now though
i can already see the flies
swarming around your reprobate mind

naked thoughts

The thief comes only to steal and kill and destroy.
My purpose is to give life in all its fullness.
John 10:10

quandra

come home

to the prodigal son
who thought it might be fun
to take your inheritance
and waste it on your merriment

on women
on alcohol
always spendin'
hanging in the pool hall

but now the money is gone
you're feeling all alone
so let me remind you
you can always come home
some say home is where the heart is
but your heart is full of garbage
so your heart might lead you wrong
i say home is where the Lord is
so when you're feeling all alone
know that you can always come home

memphis anointing

there is nothing quite like that memphis anointing
that memphis glory
that leaves me hungry
for heaven
all those saints in the pyramid
amide
God's most honorable vessels
yes those
meetings in memphis are like none other for me

it's not the crowds of people
musicals
hats
expensive, gaudy suits
long, belabored offering calls
a 30 minute wait in denny's dining hall
i could do without all
that
but there's something about that Memphis anointing
that calls me back
despite the big heads with big names with reserved
seating
leaving me
dizzy with a nose bleed
at the top of the pyramid's seating

quandra

but still i'm amide
God's most honorable vessels
yes those
powerful bishops
who usher us
to a higher level of reality
reminding me
of that pentecostal glory
that blessed this nation back on Azusa street
yes that makes it all worth it for me
that Memphis anointing
despite those free rides who lack real courtesy
you'll see me
at the meeting

yes 'cause that memphis meeting has an anointing
a glory
beyond what i could ever see
locally

naked thoughts

You are the light of the world. A city on a hill cannot be hidden. Neither do people light a lamp and put it under a bowl. Instead they put it on its stand, and it gives light to everyone in the house. In the same way, let your light shine before men, that they may see your good deeds and praise your Father in heaven.
Matthew 5:14-16

quandra

testify

this world is so big
and so dark

my candle is so dim
and so small

but just when i decide there's no use for my shine
i notice a small candle in the distance

a witness

and i think to myself
if i can see that small candle shine
then i know that someone else

can

see

mine

naked thoughts

Nehemiah said, "Go and enjoy choice food and sweet drinks, and send some to those who have nothing prepared. This day is sacred to our Lord. Do not grieve for the joy of the Lord is your strength."
Nehemiah 8:10

You have made known to me the path of life; you will fill me with joy in your presence, with eternal pleasures at your right hand.
Psalm 16:11

quandra

what is joy?

what is joy
do i have it when i'm sad
or only when i'm shoutin' glad

what is joy
is it only here when my soul is on fire
and does it leave when i'm in my trials

joy is not effervescent
but is ever present
passes understanding
there wherever I am standing

in good times
in pain
in bad times
keeping me sane

joy does not flow from my circumstance
but from God while in that holy trance
as long as I'm in His presence
i will never be joyless

naked thoughts

pick me up

daddy
can you pick me up
daddy
can you pick me up
just lift me up
onto your shoulders with your big strong hands
larger than any circumstance
and keep me from all hurt
keep me tucked away, safe with you
tell me what do so i'm never confused

daddy, you always took me to church and kept me from hurt
but then i grew up
so now daddy can't pick me up
his strength all but faded and his wisdom sometimes dated
he's not available to me to be all that i think i need
so now i'm in search of another brother who might
pick me up
pick me up

playa will you pick me up
playa will you pick me up
pick me and place me
up on your pedal stool
i'll be a fool for you playa

quandra

i'll make you happy just as long i can be
the only girl in your world
playa keep me safe with you
tell me what to do so i'm not confused
but playa doesn't hold his name in vain
he will always play the game
i begged for him to pick me
and he did
but only to hit it and quit it
leaving my love unrequited

so now daddy ain't around
and my playa can't be found
but i vaguely remembered when i came to myself
that you, Father, might be one to help
pick me up
i'm here stuck in my own muck
the pig's pen hired hand looking for someone to understand
someone to tell me what to do
so i'm not so hurt and confused

bearing the load of my sin, left hurt and abused
'cause i've given my heart to everyone but you
but every day is another chance
to rise above my circumstance
to learn to stand firm with my heart in your hand
i'm beginning to understand that trust in God is better than confidence in man

naked thoughts

so Father, will you pick me up
Father, will you pick me up
lift me up from this agony of serving me
'cause serving flesh is what left me in this mess
leaving me bleeding and confused
needing only you
in you i reach the epitome of all that you want your creation to be
so i'm no longer searching for some fallible person to affirm and define me
'cause that dependency on flesh will only blind me of your will for me
surrendering all is a must but we ought to be careful who we choose to trust
so with my hands raised and my heart lifted up
i'm asking
you
Father if you'll
pick
      me
             up

quandra

For the wages of sin is death, but the gift of God is
eternal life in Christ Jesus our Lord.
Romans 6:23

then

when i give up the ghost
my spirit returns to God
and my old body turns to dust
what then
will i be rewarded for righteousness
or condemned for my sin
what then
eternal life
will be
then

once God's angels
escort me to heaven's gate
carry my soul over the threshold
what then
rest in God's presence
will be
then

once all the saints in heaven
create a great congregation
at the close of tribulation
what then
reception of our rewards
will be
then

quandra

    the fact of such eternal bliss
    makes me wonder why you'd miss
    it for temporal pleasures and treasures
    don't you want to see
    what will be
    then

naked thoughts

contact author

vesselofhonor@trinitypublishing.org

quandra

what I've learned

sometimes

the only thing that can heal a situation is the passage of time

be patient

about the author

Quandra is a child of the Church of God in Christ. she currently lives in Oakland, California and is a member of South Bay Community Church in Fremont (an Evangelical Covenant church). Soon after receiving her Bachelors Degree in Molecular and Cell Biology from the University of California at Berkeley, she began doing research in immunogenetics at Children's Hospital of Oakland Research Institute. While doing research full-time, she studies at Holy Names College for her Masters in Business Administration. Science is her career path. Church is her heart. Poetry is her therapy.

Printed in the United States
1232800001B/115-174